TABLE OF CONTENTS

ALL TOGETHER NOW

All around the world, people come together in communities.

We live together. We grow together. We love each other.

COMMON GROUNDS

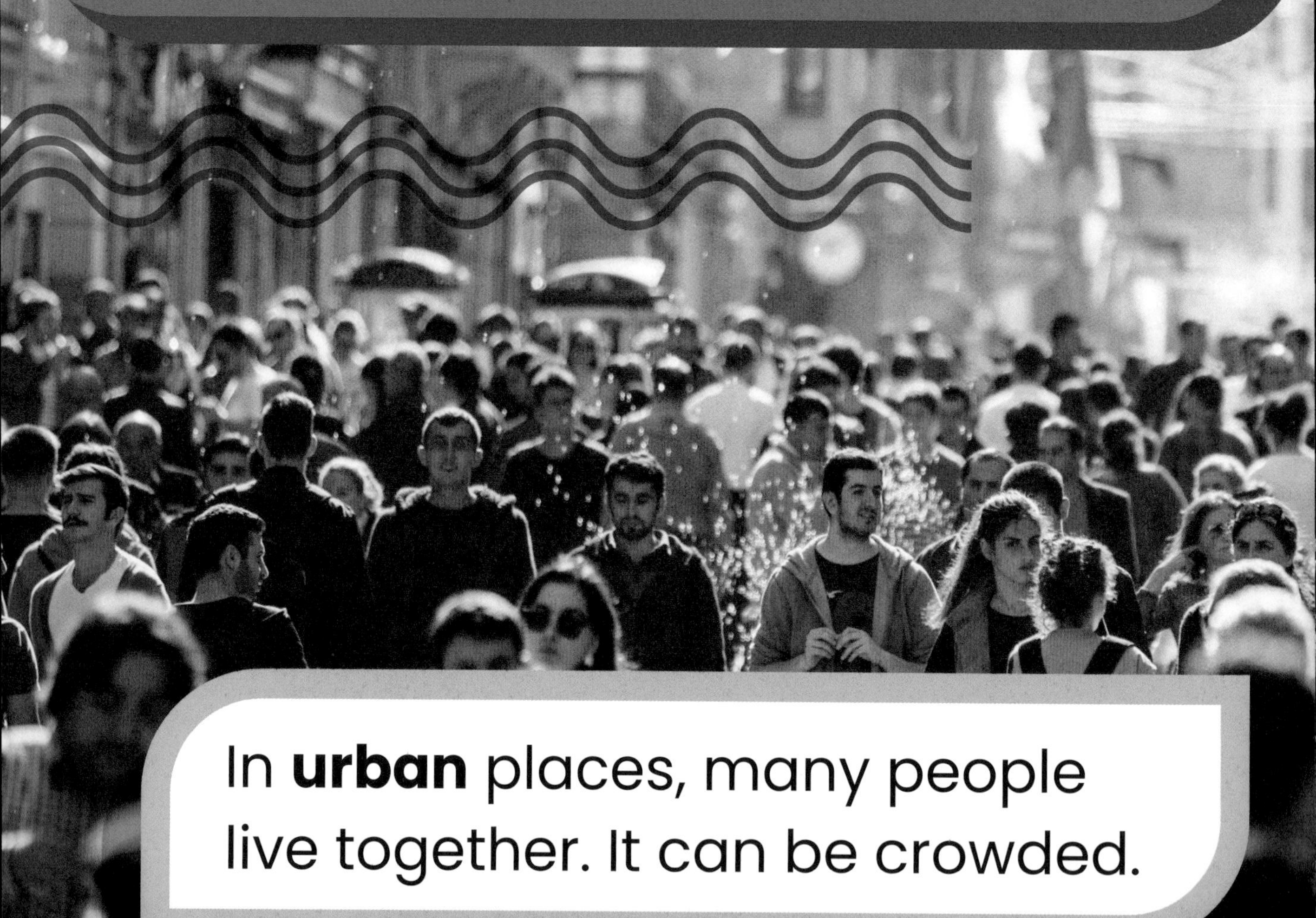

In **urban** places, many people live together. It can be crowded.

Big cities are urban places.

DID YOU KNOW?

There are around 40 million people who live in the city of Tokyo, Japan!

Suburban communities are usually close to cities.

Fewer people live here.

Rural areas are made up of mostly countryside.

There aren't as many people who live in rural areas.

GOT GROCERIES?

Rural communities do not have many stores. Gustavus, Alaska, has only one grocery store.

WE ARE FAMILY

Families are everywhere.

Every family is different.

Some families have few people.
Some families have lots of people.

DID YOU KNOW?

In many cultures, you will find **generations** of families living together, like aunts, uncles, cousins, and grandparents.

Some family members don't look alike. But all families have love.

LOVE WITHOUT LIMITS

Children can be adopted. They become part of a new family.

GO TEAM

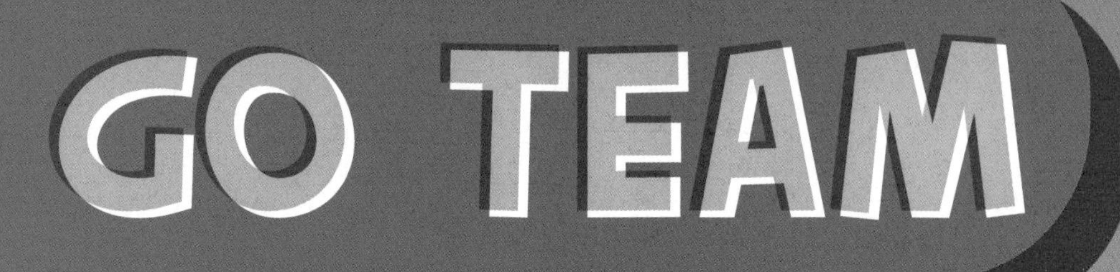

People grow together in groups.

At work, people can team up to change the world.

Friends come together to learn and play. Sometimes they play to win!

DID YOU KNOW?

More than a million children participate on a sports team in the United States.

PHOTO GLOSSARY

generation (jen-uh-RAY-shuhn): all the people born around the same time

rural (ROOR-uhl): having to do with the country or countryside

suburban (suh-BUR-buhn): having to do with a smaller community close to a city

urban (UR-buhn): having to do with a city

ACTIVITY

MY COMMUNITY

Supplies

paper
crayons
ruler

Directions

1. Using the ruler, draw a line down the middle of your paper.
2. Using the ruler, draw a line across the middle of your paper.

Fill in the Boxes:

3. Draw a picture of where you live in the top left box.
4. Draw a picture of your family in the box next to it.
5. Draw a picture of the grocery store in your community in the bottom left box.
6. Draw a picture of things you can buy at the grocery store next to it.

How many people are in your family? How many people are in your friends' families? Do you have more or less people in your family than your friends?

INDEX

ABOUT THE AUTHOR

Shantel Gobin is an urban educator. She enjoys living in Brooklyn, New York, with her family. She loves exploring and learning about different communities.

AFTER-READING ACTIVITY

With a parent, go for a walk in your community and do some research. What do you see? What do you hear? What type of community do you live in? Discuss your research with a family member.

Library of Congress PCN Data

Communities, Families, and Groups / Shantel Gobin
(Social Studies Connect)
ISBN 978-1-73165-635-3 (hard cover)(alk. paper)
ISBN 978-1-73165-608-7 (soft cover)
ISBN 978-1-73165-617-9 (eBook)
ISBN 978-1-73165-626-1 (ePub)
Library of Congress Control Number: 2022943044

Rourke Educational Media
Printed in the United States of America
01-0372311937

www.rourkebooks.com

Edited by: Catherine Malaski
Cover design by: Morgan Burnside
Interior design by: Morgan Burnside

Photo Credits: Cover, page 1: ©Pollyana Ventura/ Getty Images, ©Siri Stafford/ Getty Images, ©pixelra
Shutterstock.com; Cover, pages 1, 16: ©monkeybusinessimages/ Getty Images; pages 4-5: ©Mesquita
Shutterstock.com; page 5: ©Toystory/ Shutterstock.com; pages 6-7: ©filadendron/ Getty Images;
page 7: ©Sean Pavone/ Shutterstock.com; pages 8-9: ©Konstantin L/ Shutterstock.com; pages 10-11:
©omersukrugoksu/ Getty Images; page 11: ©wildatart/ Getty Images; page 12: ©vichie81/
Shutterstock.com, ©Vane Nunes/ Shutterstock.com; page 13: ©pixelrain/ Shutterstock.com; pages 14-
©LanaG/ Shutterstock.com; page 15: ©szefei/ Shutterstock.com, ©NDAB Creativity/
Shutterstock.com; page 17: ©NDAB Creativity/ Shutterstock.com, ©enigma_images/ Getty Images; pag
18: ©Sergey Novikov/ Shutterstock.com; page 19: ©LightField Studios/ Shutterstock.com; pages 20-21
©Marcelo Murillo/ Shutterstock.com; page 21: ©Daisy-Daisy/ Getty Images, ©Jupiterimages/ Getty
Images; page 22: ©JamesBrey/ Getty Images, ©photovs/ Getty Images, ©peeterv/ Getty Images, ©fizk
Shutterstock.com